CW01081972

being a **small group** leader

Richard Sweatman

SYDNEY · YOUNGSTOWN

Matthias Media
(St Matthias Press Ltd ACN 067 558 365)
Email: info@matthiasmedia.com.au
Internet: www.matthiasmedia.com.au
Please visit our website for current postal and telephone contact information.

Matthias Media (USA)
Email: sales@matthiasmedia.com
Internet: www.matthiasmedia.com
Please visit our website for current postal and telephone contact information.

ISBN 978 1 925424 32 4

Cover design and typesetting by Lankshear Design.

Contents

Introduction   5

1. Knowledge of God   11

2. Character   25

3. Teaching ability   33

4. Encouragement of others   43

5. Team leadership   53

6. Being a competent Growth Group leader   61

Introduction

Small groups (or home groups) shouldn't really work at all. We take ten to twelve flawed and sinful Christians, put them under the leadership of an equally flawed and sinful Christian leader, and get them to study the Bible—which is full of things that can be hard to understand or even controversial. On top of this we expect people to love and care for each other while sharing just how flawed and sinful they are. When you put it like this, small groups sound more like a formula for dysfunctionality, conflict and discouragement. They shouldn't really work at all.

But by God's kindness and the work of his Spirit, they do work. Despite the limitations, the small group activities of Bible study, prayer and relating together *do* grow people as Christians. Sure, there are sometimes people who seem to be spiritually treading water or drifting away; but on the whole most people in a group will have grown together as Christians over the course of a year. Somehow they will have become a bit more like Jesus.

Being a leader in this awkward set-up is both challenging and rewarding. It's *challenging* because it's hard work. Leading involves preparing studies, making phone calls and being concerned for people. Moreover, in leadership we come face to face with many of our own sins and weaknesses. But it's also *rewarding*. Even though we are flawed and sinful God does use us to grow his people. Most leaders can look back over a year in leadership and see how their group members have actually grown as Christians together.

But what makes someone a good small group leader? Is it enough to have the desire and availability? These things are obviously necessary (1 Timothy 3:1 talks about someone 'aspiring' to be an overseer), but the Bible has a lot more to say about what makes someone suited to leadership. There are lists of qualities, job descriptions and teaching about what leadership involves, and much of this can be applied to leading small groups. As I've trained and appointed small group leaders I've found it helpful to organize these qualities under five areas or headings. I've called them the 'five core competencies' of small group leading.

'Competencies' may seem like an odd choice of word at first, because we often use it synonymously with the word 'skills'. But I actually mean competencies in a broader sense—that is, all the things about a person that make them an appropriate person for the job. Those things generally mean *more* than just their skills. For example, a ship's captain may have all the training and seamanship skills needed, but if he is a drunkard, he's not the one you want at the helm. As you'll see in a moment, issues of personal character very much come within what I mean by 'competence'.

And why 'five'? Well, five seems about the right number; besides, any more and nobody can remember them. And it's also five because from the Bible and my experience as a pastor these are the 'core' competencies—they are vital for leading. But it's worth highlighting here and now that 'competencies' are about being capable and growing in each area—not about being perfect, or even outstanding for that matter. If we wait for people to reach perfection before they start leading, we're going to have a lot of leaderless groups! If you are already leading then you will no doubt already have realized that you are not perfect. And sometimes that can have us question whether we've got what it takes to keep going. As you read this book you will be encouraged to keep growing, to keep striving and to keep trusting God to grow his people through your ministry.

Listing these leadership qualities helps us to think about what leading involves, how we're going in these areas, and what goals we can set. It's also helpful for pastors as we think about appointing people for leadership.

So what are they? The five core competencies of leading small groups are:

1. Knowledge of God
2. Character
3. Teaching ability
4. Encouragement of others
5. Team leadership

Hopefully, as we look at each competency you'll be encouraged to see that you're doing okay in some areas and you have room for growth in others. At the end of each chapter there will be some questions to help you reflect on what you've read and set some goals. I want reading this book to be a helpful and practical experience.

Before launching into the self-reflection and goal setting, one thing that's important to remember is God's grace. That's why in the diagram below the five core competencies sit in a 'framework of grace'. The Bible teaches that not only are we saved by grace, but everything to do with ministry (including small group leading) is about grace. Our ministries (whatever they are) are given to us by grace (1 Cor 15:10; 2 Cor 4:1) and whatever godliness or gifts we have are also by God's grace (2 Thess 1:3; Rom 12:6-8). Any ministry 'success' is by grace (1 Cor 3:5-7), and even ministry 'failure' is a kindness from God that teaches us dependence on him (2 Cor 1:8-10). Remembering this will help us not to despair if we're struggling in some areas and not to be proud if we're doing well in others. Rather, we can be people who give thanks to God for everything and see every weakness as an opportunity for prayer.

Understanding grace should also drive us to be people of prayer for those in our small groups. *No matter how 'competent' we are as leaders, those we lead will not grow without the Holy Spirit being at work in them.* It is, in other words, *God* who gives the growth (1 Cor 3:6-7). So we must express this in our regular and faithful prayers for people throughout the week. All that follows in this book presumes this undergirding commitment on our part to prayer and to asking God to be at work. Indeed, our prayerfulness flows as a natural outworking of our *knowledge of God* as the sovereign ruler, and from our *character* as faithful and dependent leaders.

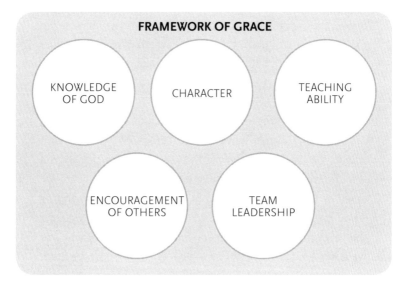

FRAMEWORK OF GRACE

KNOWLEDGE OF GOD

CHARACTER

TEACHING ABILITY

ENCOURAGEMENT OF OTHERS

TEAM LEADERSHIP

'Growth Groups'

You might have noticed that so far in this book I've been referring to the groups we're leading as 'small groups'. Perhaps your church has another name for them, like 'home groups' or 'connect groups'. But I've started off using the somewhat generic term 'small groups' because I think most church people will know the sort of thing I'm talking about.

Now perhaps it doesn't matter what we call them, so long as there's not confusion about what we mean. But on the other hand, it *can* matter, because what we *call* things often shapes our view of them and communicates what we think and believe about their nature and purpose.

If that's the case, maybe 'small group' is actually a slightly ineffective name. It doesn't communicate much about the group's purpose—only its size (and it's even a bit vague about that).

Now I don't want to be overly prescriptive about it, but to signal that the sort of groups I am talking about have a goal and purpose, I'm going to call them 'Growth Groups' from this point on in the book. And I do that because I believe that our groups exist to help people *grow* in Christ and towards maturity in Christ over time. And also because it's always good if groups grow as they work together to make new disciples of Christ and welcome new people into their group.

I'll say a little more along the way about what a Growth Group is for. But I want to encourage you to think more deeply about this key question of the group's *purpose*: what are you seeking to do when you get together? Your role as a leader is very much determined by the overarching goal for your group: just where are you leading people as a leader? This is definitely something you need to wrestle with deeply... with your Bible open. To that end, I want to encourage you to make use of *The Small Group and the Vine*, a Growth Group leaders' training course that explores this issue in greater depth than I will be doing in this book.

Questions

- At first glance, what do you think about the 'five core competencies' of Growth Group leading?

- Why is it important to remember God's grace as we think about all this?

- How are you feeling about Growth Group leadership?

1. Knowledge of God

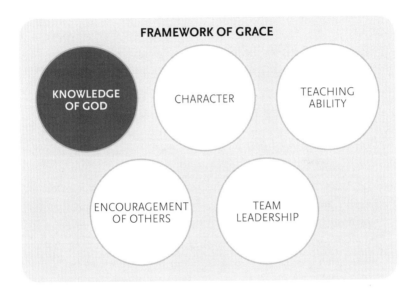

The first area of competency for Growth Group leaders is *knowledge of God*. From prison, Paul wrote about this to Timothy:

> ...the gospel, for which I was appointed a preacher and apostle and teacher, which is why I suffer as I do. But I am not ashamed, for *I know whom I have believed*, and I am convinced that he is able to guard until that day what has been entrusted to me. (2 Tim 1:10-12)

You can see that Paul's knowledge of God helps him endure suffering and persevere in his ministry. Even though we might not end up in prison, the principle is the same for us: *knowing God* is at the heart of who we are and what we do.

But what does it mean to know God? Do we need to become

Bible experts or reach some new spiritual state of intimacy with God? A topic like this raises all sorts of questions. Fortunately, it's not too hard to explain.

The knowledge we're talking about can be summed up under four headings.

Relational knowledge

It's important as Christians and leaders that we don't just know *about* God; we must actually *know God*. Our knowledge must be part of a genuine relationship with him. It's like the difference between knowing the Prime Minister and knowing your friend—both kinds of knowledge involve information, but only one involves a personal relationship.

Thankfully, God takes the initiative in making himself known to us. It's only by grace that we come into a personal relationship with him. In fact, the Bible sometimes reverses the way we usually think about knowing God: "But now that you have come to know God, or rather to be known by God..." (Gal 4:9a).

Clearly we're not talking about a detached academic knowledge of God, but rather a warm and personal knowledge that's part of a genuine relationship. Knowledge like this means things like faith, trust, love and joy. It will flow on to prayer and a desire to know God better.

Scriptural knowledge

True knowledge of God will not only be relational, it will also be *scriptural*. The Bible is the way God makes himself known, so it's important that our knowledge of him comes from the Bible and fits with the Bible. You can find this theme everywhere, but Psalm 119 talks about this especially. The whole psalm is worth reading, but verses 129-132 give a good taste of the idea:

Your testimonies are wonderful;
    therefore my souls keeps them.
The unfolding of your words gives light;
    it imparts understanding to the simple.
I open my mouth and pant,
    because I long for your commandments.
Turn to me and be gracious to me,
    as is your way with those who love your name.
(Ps 119:129-132)

The psalmist clearly loves God and longs to read and understand God's word to know him better.

You can see how knowing our Bibles well is not about being 'Bible experts' for the sake of it. It's part of how we continually grow in our knowledge of God. For Growth Group leaders this will mean some competency in being able to read and understand the Bible (this is often called *exegesis*). It will also mean at least a basic understanding of how the Bible fits together and makes up one coherent whole (this is often called *biblical theology*).

Thoughtful knowledge

Knowledge of God is not just about becoming familiar with the Bible. We are also called to *think* about God and his word. You can see this in the way the writer to the Hebrews challenges his readers:

About this we have much to say, and it is hard to explain, since you have become dull of hearing. For though by this time you ought to be teachers, you need someone to teach you again the basic principles of the oracles of God. You need milk, not solid food, for everyone who lives on milk is unskilled in the word of righteousness,

since he is a child. But solid food is for the mature, for
those who have their powers of discernment trained
by constant practice to distinguish good from evil.
(Heb 5:11-14)

Basic and simple knowledge is good, but the writer wants them
to learn and think and grow. So we want to have a deepening,
thoughtful knowledge of God (this is sometimes called *doctrine*).
It's about understanding God more and connecting ideas in the
Bible. Growth Group leaders do not need to be tertiary trained
experts, but they should have some competency in doctrine as
part of their knowledge of God. Titus 1:9 says that the elder
must "hold firm to the trustworthy word as taught".

So as we know God, we want to be thoughtful about the
Bible and hold to the "trustworthy word as taught".

Practical knowledge

According to the Bible, true knowledge of God will affect our
lives; it will be *practical*. James says in his letter:

But be doers of the word, and not hearers only, deceiving
yourselves. For if anyone is a hearer of the word and
not a doer, he is like a man who looks intently at his
natural face in a mirror. For he looks at himself and goes
away and at once forgets what he was like. But the one
who looks into the perfect law, the law of liberty, and
perseveres, being no hearer who forgets but a doer who
acts, he will be blessed in his doing. (Jas 1:22-25)

You can see from this passage how important it is that our
knowledge of God from the Bible translates into action. Bible
reading skills and doctrine don't mean much if they don't
transform us—if our lives are more or less the same as everyone else in the world around us.

So knowledge of God must be practical. It will mean wrestling with how to live and making real changes to our thinking, our speech and our actions.

To sum up then, the sort of knowledge we're talking about is relational, scriptural, thoughtful and practical. It's a genuine and exciting knowledge of our great God and creator. It's actually something we'd want for everyone at church, whether or not they are in leadership.

Why it matters

Knowledge of God is great, and God is God and he deserves to be known, loved and worshipped! But why is it especially important for leaders? There are at least three reasons the Bible gives for this.

1. Leaders set an example

We will see in the next chapter how leaders set an example for people in their Christian character. The same is true for knowledge of God. Knowing God is essential for every Christian and so it's important that leaders live this out and model it to group members. Even if there were no other reasons for leaders to know God, this would be enough to make it a priority.

2. Leaders teach

A second reason leaders need to know God well is that leaders teach (I'll say more about this in chapter 3). Teaching involves the sharing of knowledge, so obviously leaders need to have some knowledge to share. Paul compares a leader to a worker with the Bible as his tool:

> Do your best to present yourself to God as one approved, a worker who has no need to be ashamed, rightly handling the word of truth. (2 Tim 2:15)

To be effective teachers, leaders need to know the Bible and have sound doctrine.

3. Leaders protect

A third reason is that teachers need to protect the people they lead from false teaching. False teaching is a constant threat to Christians according to the Bible (e.g. Col 2:16-23; 2 Thess 2:1-3; 2 Tim 4:3-4; 2 Peter 2). Sometimes this is explained as Satan's work to ruin people's faith in Jesus (Rev 2:20-24). Into this hostile environment Jesus has provided teachers to help us stand firm (Eph 4:7-16). So a competent leader will know doctrine and the Bible well enough to be able to do this. Paul puts it this way in his letter to Titus:

> He must hold firm to the trustworthy word as taught, so that he may be able to give instruction in sound doctrine and also to rebuke those who contradict it. (Titus 1:9)

The leader with Bible knowledge and understanding (i.e. sound doctrine) will be able to recognize when people teach wrong ideas, and challenge them.

It takes some wisdom to know when an idea is wrong or dangerous and what sort of steps need to be taken. Thankfully, this wisdom is something that itself comes from knowing God better. The Bible also gives guidance about figuring out the difficulties of false teaching (e.g. 2 Tim 2:23-26; Titus 3:9-10). And God will have usually provided the church with more experienced pastors who are able to help in these tricky situations.

So to sum up: knowing God is crucial for leaders because they set an example, teach others and protect the people they are leading from false teaching. A leader who is competent and growing in this area will, under God, be a great blessing to the people he or she leads.

Before we look at practical ways to grow in this area, it's worth noting how connected this is to character. Knowing God changes our character, and a humble and godly character will lead us to want to know God more. There's a great verse that puts the two ideas together:

> Keep a close watch on yourself and on the teaching.
> Persist in this, for by so doing you will save both yourself
> and your hearers. (1 Tim 4:16)

Our life and doctrine really do matter—not just for ourselves, but for the people we lead and teach as well.

Growing in our knowledge of God

Hopefully this chapter has served as motivation to continue to grow in your knowledge and understanding of God. Here are some practical ways to do this.

1. Prayer

Prayer is a great place to start because it reminds us of God's grace. Knowledge of God is something that God gives us, and prayer reminds us of that. So the best thing to do is ask God to help us grow in our knowledge of him. Look at this great promise in James:

> If any of you lacks wisdom, let him ask God, who gives
> generously to all without reproach, and it will be given
> him. (Jas 1:5)

I've always loved this verse because I constantly feel like I lack the wisdom to manage life, let alone lead other Christians. It has regularly encouraged me to pray to God and ask for wisdom.

2. Bible reading

There's no way around this. Knowing God better means reading our Bibles. Unfortunately, sometimes we don't read as much as we'd like to or know we should. I think the best way to grow in this is to figure out your theological convictions about Bible reading and establish some good habits that reflect those convictions. Let's look at both of these elements in turn.

A theological conviction about Bible reading is something that motivates you to read. Ideally it will be something that you can put in your own words that makes sense to you. There are many different reasons to read the Bible, but usually there'll be one or two that resonate deeply with us. I'm fairly logical and clinical by personality so a motivation that works for me is: "God has said that Bible reading is good for me, so I'm going to do it". You might find other theological ideas more motivating, such as our love of God or the work of the Spirit. The important thing is to find a theological motivation that you can put into your own words, believe and act on.

The second way to grow as a Bible reader is to establish some good habits. Here are 10 tips you can try:

1. **Read regularly.** Try to find times in the day that work for you. It's different for everyone.
2. **Start small.** Don't set goals that are unrealistic. Just get reading, even if that's only a few verses or a paragraph three or four days a week. As you build habits, the chances are that you'll start to read more and more.
3. **Pray before and after you read.** It's great to pray for God's help in understanding, and then pray that God would help you apply what you just read. You can pray even if you don't feel like you've understood everything. For example, you might pray: "Dear God, thank you that you were in control

of what was happening with the Israelites. Please help me to remember that you are in control even now."

4. **Read big and small sections.** Sometimes it's great to read just a few verses and think deeply about them. Sometimes it's great to read large chunks and let the words and ideas wash over you. Both are good.

5. **Read with other people.** Try reading the Bible with friends or your spouse or family. Invite other people to encourage you in your Bible reading and ask you how you're going.

6. **Keep track of your progress.** Most people find it encouraging to tick off chapters in a Bible reading plan (they are easy to find online).

7. **Try using different Bible reading guides.** There are guides from Matthias Media or the Good Book Company (see footnote 1 in chapter 2). You could also try making notes about what you've been reading. Some people even highlight verses in their Bibles and jot things in the margins.

8. **Try listening to an audio Bible.** Some people do this during their daily commute.

9. **Read even when you don't feel like it.** Satan sometimes tricks us by getting us to think we need to be in 'the right mood' to read the Bible. This is getting things the wrong way around. Reading the Bible will help your mood, so don't let Satan trick you—just get into it and read.

10. **Use a paper Bible.** It's handy to have our Bible on our phone but there's something about having the whole Bible in front of you. It helps us remember that every verse is part of a chapter, which is part of a book, which is part of the whole Bible, which is the unified message of God.

3. Theological reading

Good Christian books will help us grow in our knowledge of God. They don't do this by adding anything to the Bible—it's still the Bible alone that reveals God. Rather, good books help us understand the Bible better and get more out of it when we read. Many Christians can look back and see how they've been pushed along in their Christian maturity by good books.

I love books and reading so I need to be aware of my own personal bias, but I think reading is better than listening to sermons online. I find I am passive as a listener but active as a reader as I seek to understand and engage with what the author is saying. For me reading is harder work, but better value.

What if you're 'not a reader'? That's okay; some people naturally enjoy reading more than others. But it doesn't mean we don't read at all. Ideally, a desire to grow in maturity and serve the people we lead will spur us on to increase our understanding by reading some helpful Christian books.

If you're just starting out, you're best off taking on short books that are easy to read. I'd suggest setting a modest goal of reading two or three over the next twelve months. It might also be worth reading with someone else who can encourage you to keep going. Catch up with each other regularly to discuss a chapter or two and keep each other accountable to finish the book.

Here are some good books for anyone starting out in Christian book reading:

- Some children's resources could be a good start if reading is something you generally avoid. *The Big Picture Story Bible* by David Helm (Crossway), *The Gospel Story Bible* by Marty Machowski (New Growth Press) and *The Biggest Story* by Kevin de Young (Crossway) all show how the whole Bible fits together as one big story. (You can pretend you're buying it for your kids or for kids' ministry.)

- *Gospel and Kingdom* by Graeme Goldsworthy (Paternoster Press). This is a biblical theology classic. It explains how nearly everything in the Bible has got to do with God's people living in God's place under God's rule.
- *God's Big Picture* by Vaughan Roberts (InterVarsity Press). Vaughan Roberts loved *Gospel and Kingdom* but wanted to teach the ideas even more simply and clearly to his congregation. This book came out of the teaching course he ran.
- *Know and Tell the Gospel* by John Chapman (Matthias Media). John Chapman was a giant among Australian Christians and left a huge legacy in excellent teaching of both evangelism and preaching. This book not only explains the gospel clearly but offers a lot of encouragement to explain it well to others.

If you enjoy reading then there are plenty more great Christian books to read. After a while you'll realize that there are different categories of Christian books. It's worth reading from each category and reading old books as well as new. Here's a basic list to get started (in addition to the ones listed above), but it's worth asking your pastor about extra ideas.

Biblical theology
- *According to Plan: An Introduction to Biblical Theology* by Graeme Goldsworthy (InterVarsity Press)

General doctrine
- *Big Truths for Young Hearts: Teaching and Learning the Greatness of God* by Bruce Ware (Crossway)
- *The Everlasting God* by DB Knox (Matthias Media)
- *Know the Truth: A Handbook of Christian Belief* by Bruce Milne (InterVarsity Press)

- *Concise Theology: A Guide to Historic Christian Beliefs* by JI Packer (Tyndale House)

Specific doctrines
- *The Cross of Christ* by John Stott (InterVarsity Press)
- *Knowing God* by JI Packer (InterVarsity Press)
- *Guidance and the Voice of God* by Phillip Jensen and Tony Payne (Matthias Media)
- *Prayer and the Voice of God* by Phillip Jensen and Tony Payne (Matthias Media)
- *God's Good Design* by Claire Smith (Matthias Media)
- *The Essence of the Reformation* by Kirsten Birkett (Matthias Media)

There are lots more great books I could suggest but I don't want to get carried away here. The point is that we read and read well.

4. Theological training

If you're up for it then some sort of theological training will help you grow in your knowledge of God. Correspondence courses can be a convenient way to do this—for example, the courses available from Moore College in Sydney. The first subject of the Moore College course is 'Introduction to the Bible', which many have found to be very helpful. You could also ask your pastor for recommendations.

Conclusion

So there you have four ways to grow in knowledge of God—a knowledge that is relational, scriptural, thoughtful and practical. But remember God's grace! He is the one who, by his Spirit, will bring about growth in us. Hopefully any further growth will lead to greater humility, not pride.

Questions

- Try to express the four ways of describing true knowledge of God in your own words (relational, scriptural, thoughtful and practical). What do you think of these? Do you naturally tend to emphasize one or two of these at the expense of others?

- Why is it important for leaders to be competent in their knowledge of God?

- What motivates you theologically in Bible reading?

- What practical tips did you find helpful? Can you make a plan to put them into practice?

- What Christian book would you like to read next?

- Write down some goals in the table below for growing in your knowledge of God. I've included an example.

Goal	Plan	Time period
Grow in my understanding of biblical theology.	Read *According to Plan* by Graeme Goldsworthy. Find a friend to read and discuss it with.	Aim to finish it in two months. Start today!

Being a Small Group Leader

2. Character

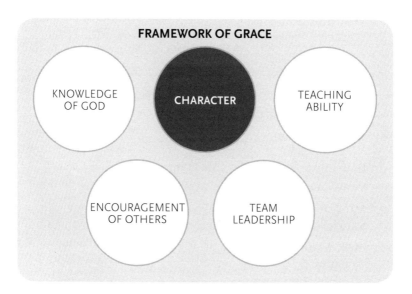

FRAMEWORK OF GRACE

KNOWLEDGE OF GOD

CHARACTER

TEACHING ABILITY

ENCOURAGEMENT OF OTHERS

TEAM LEADERSHIP

The second area of competency is character. Character is that quality of being tested in life and proving solid. We see this in Romans 5:

> Not only that, but we rejoice in our sufferings, knowing that suffering produces endurance, and endurance produces character, and character produces hope...
> (vv. 3-4)

Character includes things like love, patience, self-control, kindness and sexual purity, but the Bible talks about it so much and in so many different ways that it's hard to sum it up! One of the catch-all terms for character is being "above reproach" (1 Tim 3:2; Titus 1:6). This is not talking about being sinless (only

Jesus managed that), but rather a level of Christian growth and maturity that means someone can't be accused of a serious sin. This is especially any sin that would damage the reputation of Jesus. Paul goes on in his letters to Titus and Timothy to be more specific about what this means—talking about things like gentleness and avoiding drunkenness (1 Tim 3:1-7; Titus 1:6-8).

Why it matters

There are three main reasons that Growth Group leaders should be of sound character.

1. Our example

In the Bible, Jesus is clearly held up as an *example* for us to follow (John 13:14-16; 1 Cor 11:1; 1 Pet 2:21). He will always be the perfect model of godliness. But Jesus isn't the only example for us to follow—Christian leaders are also meant to be examples to the people they lead. We see this in the way Paul writes to Timothy:

> Let no-one despise you for your youth, but set the
> believers an example in speech, in conduct, in love, in
> faith, in purity. (1 Tim 4:12)

He says a similar thing to Titus (Titus 2:7) and also speaks about himself as an example (1 Cor 4:16, 11:1; Phil 3:17; 2 Thess 3:7; see also Heb 13:7). It's clear that God wants his leaders to set an example in their character and have others follow them.

So as we consider our character, one question that's worth asking ourselves regularly is whether it would be a good thing if our group members became more like us during the course of a year. That can be a confronting question to ask, and we need to be realistic as we ask it, but it can certainly help us focus in on areas of our character we need to work on.

2. The demands of ministry

Character is also important for leaders because of the demands of ministry. Ministry is hard work. It means loving and serving people week in and week out. It can also mean dealing with different kinds of conflict. We see this in the way Paul talks to Timothy:

> So flee youthful passions and pursue righteousness, faith, love, and peace, along with those who call on the Lord from a pure heart. Have nothing to do with foolish, ignorant controversies; you know that they breed quarrels. And the Lord's servant must not be quarrelsome but kind to everyone, able to teach, patiently enduring evil, correcting his opponents with gentleness. God may perhaps grant them repentance leading to a knowledge of the truth, and they may come to their senses and escape from the snare of the devil, after being captured by him to do his will.
> (2 Tim 2:22-26)

This passage shows us that in the midst of quarrels or opposition Timothy must show kindness and gentleness. You can see why character matters at this point!

So it's worth reflecting on how our character might hold up when we need to love and serve people who could be hard to love, or others who just need greater understanding and care. How will we cope with some of the demands of ministry? Do we need to grow in compassion or patience? Do we need to put off anger or bitterness? Leading a Growth Group can be challenging, so whatever maturity we have in our character will help.

3. Our teaching

The third reason our character matters as leaders is that the impact of our teaching depends on it. The impact of the message can be affected by the integrity of the messenger (or the lack of it). As Paul points out in Titus 2:10, our godly behaviour in the presence of others can "adorn the doctrine of God our Saviour" (or not).

When we lead a Growth Group we will be teaching the Bible and calling on people to believe it and live it out. But if we are not doing this ourselves we would be hypocrites without integrity. That would be a tragedy, not only for our own leadership, but because it would mean people in our group might follow our example and not take God's word seriously either. So it's really important that our character is solid as we teach others, and that we do our best to rid ourselves of hypocrisy (1 Pet 2:1).

One way to think about this is to reflect on how we act outside of our Christian circles. The Bible talks about being "well thought of by outsiders" (1 Tim 3:7). It's helpful to ask ourselves, "How would our work colleagues react if they found out we were in leadership at church?" Would that reflect well on church and the gospel? If not, then there are probably areas of Christian character we need to work on.

There are other reasons character is important but these three—our example, the demands of ministry and the impact of our teaching—are why Growth Group leaders should be 'competent' in this area. However, as we consider character, it's crucial that we continue to remember that we are living under God's grace. This is not about earning our salvation or being better than others. Growing in our character is God's kindness to us. Any progress we've made should lead us to give thanks to him. Any weaknesses should drive us to prayer.

Growing in our character

There are no great secrets as to how to grow in our character. The Bible teaches that much of our growth happens through the Spirit of God working through Bible reading, prayer and godly Christian encouragement and relationships. The challenge for us as we seek to grow is to be honest with ourselves and repent of sins we'd rather hang on to.

For someone contemplating leadership, though, here are a few things worth considering:

1. **Get your Bible reading back on track.** We all go through dry times but long-term neglect of Bible reading won't do much for our character. There are lots of tips, strategies and guides that can help us with our Bible reading.[1] As mentioned in the previous chapter, pastors and friends are also great resources—they can often give us advice and keep us accountable.

2. **Pray.** God is the one who brings about growth in us so it makes sense to pray to him. Paul tells the Ephesians:

    > [Pray] at all times in the Spirit, with all prayer and supplication. To that end, keep alert with all perseverance, making supplication for all the saints... (Eph 6:18)

    Regularly bring specific requests about things you would like to change about your character before God. God loves to answer these prayers.

3. **Invite others to help you grow.** Sin and immaturity are like fungus: they thrive in the dark. It's much better to share your sins, weaknesses and struggles with someone you can trust. This could be your spouse, a friend or a leader at church. Give them permission to ask hard questions and give you advice. Ask them to pray for you and be willing to

---

1   See for example Matthias Media's *Daily Reading Bible* booklets or *Explore* from the Good Book Company.

pray for them. In this way you can partner with others in growing in character.

4. **Rejoice in suffering.** There's another more surprising and painful thing God uses to bring about maturity in his people, and that's suffering. As Romans 5 says:

> Not only that, but we rejoice in our sufferings, knowing that suffering produces endurance, and endurance produces character, and character produces hope... (vv. 3-4)

Suffering is usually due to something beyond our control and thankfully we can leave it up to God as to when and how we might suffer. However, sometimes we consciously avoid suffering by making moral compromises. For example, we might avoid workplace unpopularity by conforming to the office culture. In these cases we need to change urgently, be godly, and endure whatever suffering might come. God promises that painful experiences will bring growth in our character.

Conclusion

Character is a clear biblical priority for Christian leaders. For most of us it's not hard to spot areas in our life we could work on. Thankfully, by God's grace, we can and should expect to grow in our character as we grow in Christ. Hopefully that growth will also prepare some of us to step into leadership, ready to (humbly) lead by example, face the demands of ministry and do nothing to detract from our teaching.

Questions

- Why is character important for Growth Group leading?

- Read 1 Timothy 3 and look carefully at what it means to be "above reproach" (v. 2). How are you going with this? Are there areas you need to work on?

- How are you going in prayer and Bible reading?

- Would it be a good thing if the people in your group became more like you over the course of the year? If not, why not?

- What would people outside your Christian circles think if they learned you were a leader at church?

- Who could you talk to about your character and who would pray for you and help you grow?

- What experience have you had with suffering? Has this brought about growth in any way?

- Write down some goals for growing in your character. Again, I've included an example.

Goal	Plan	Time period
Learn to control my anger.	Look up some good verses on anger and memorize one or two of them. Confess to God and ask that he would change me. Talk with a friend.	Make a start today. Talk with a friend in a month about how it's going.

3. Teaching ability

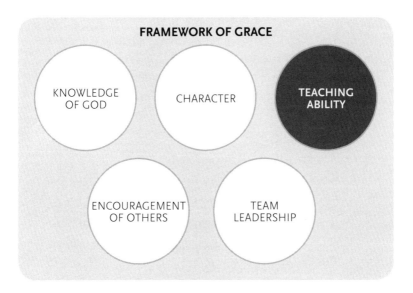

FRAMEWORK OF GRACE

KNOWLEDGE OF GOD

CHARACTER

TEACHING ABILITY

ENCOURAGEMENT OF OTHERS

TEAM LEADERSHIP

In the introduction I identified five areas in which Growth Group leaders need some level of competency. The previous chapters have covered the most important two: character and knowledge of God. These areas get the most attention in the Bible whenever leadership is talked about. The next three areas of competency—teaching ability, encouragement of others and team leadership—don't get quite the same emphasis, but nevertheless are still important in Growth Group leading. Thankfully, growing in character and knowledge of God will usually lead to growth in these other areas too.

The area of competency for this chapter is teaching ability. Teaching is helping people to learn things. In Christian ministry it's about explaining truth from the Bible and helping people read and understand things for themselves. Growth Group leaders are not merely facilitators or discussion leaders but teachers of God's word.

Paul includes the ability to teach in his description of leaders in 1 Timothy:

> The saying is trustworthy: If anyone aspires to the office of overseer, he desires a noble task. Therefore an overseer must be above reproach, the husband of one wife, sober-minded, self-controlled, respectable, hospitable, able to teach... (1 Tim 3:1-2)

It's only a brief mention but it stands out because it's pretty much the only skill in amongst a long list of character qualities. He says something similar in 2 Timothy:

> And the Lord's servant must not be quarrelsome but kind to everyone, able to teach, patiently enduring evil... (2 Tim 2:24)

We can also see the importance of teaching in the way Paul talks about it as something Timothy and Titus are to be doing in their ministries:

> Command and teach these things. Let no-one despise you for your youth, but set the believers an example in speech, in conduct, in love, in faith, in purity. Until I come, devote yourself to the public reading of Scripture, to exhortation, to teaching. (1 Tim 4:11-13)

> But as for you, teach what accords with sound doctrine. Older men are to be sober-minded, dignified, self-controlled, sound in faith, in love, and in steadfastness. Older women likewise are to be reverent in behaviour,

not slanderers or slaves to much wine. They are to teach what is good... (Titus 2:1-3)

It is clear that teaching is a significant part of a Growth Group leader's ministry and something they should be able to do.

But what does it actually mean to be able to teach? How can we describe it? In one sense it's pretty instinctive: we've usually sat under good teachers at church and Growth Groups and can recognize good teaching when we see it. I think there are at least four qualities that can be seen in a competent teacher (especially in regard to Growth Group leading). Take a look and see if they fit with your experience.

Qualities of a competent teacher

1. An awareness of others

A good teacher will be aware of how the people in their group are going—especially in the midst of the study. They'll be able to pick up if people are distracted or engaged, confused or comprehending, bored or challenged. They'll be able to pick up on the verbal or non-verbal cues and respond appropriately for the sake of the group. For example, they might repeat or rephrase a question if people are struggling, or press on to application if people are understanding ideas well.

2. An ability to let the group discover things for themselves

A competent teacher, especially in the Bible study format, will be able to encourage the group to discover things for themselves. Growth Group leading is not about giving a sermon. A good leader will be able to ask questions and leave space for people to think and discuss answers. They'll also encourage people when they are on the right track.

A good study guide (either pre-written or the leader's own)

will provide the basic questions for a study, but a leader should be able to supply a few extra questions on the fly to keep things moving along.

3. An ability to explain things

Even though Growth Group leading is mostly about helping people learn things for themselves, a capable teacher will be able to explain things from the Bible. This can be as simple as rephrasing someone's answer in a helpful way or summing up the group discussion. At other times, particularly with difficult sections of the Bible, the leader might need to explain to the group what they think the verse or passage means. This doesn't mean Growth Group leaders need to be as capable as the senior pastor, but they should be able to explain truth from the Bible in a way that's reasonably clear and helpful for their group members.

4. Creativity and a sense of fun

We all appreciate teachers who go to some effort to make learning fun. This is the same for Growth Group leading. Creativity in Bible teaching really helps people to enjoy learning and applying the Bible. This often means making the most of different learning styles in the group and asking questions that involve drawing, acting or creating things.

Why it matters

The teaching ability of the leader matters in a Growth Group because people grow by learning. Hopefully, most people will be growing through their own Bible reading and thinking—we don't want people to be solely dependent on teachers. But God does have a place for teachers who explain God's word and help the church to grow. Paul outlines this in Ephesians 4:

And he [Jesus] gave the apostles, the prophets, the evangelists, the shepherds and teachers, to equip the saints for the work of ministry, for building up the body of Christ, until we all attain to the unity of the faith and of the knowledge of the Son of God, to mature manhood, to the measure of the stature of the fullness of Christ, so that we may no longer be children, tossed to and fro by the waves and carried about by every wind of doctrine, by human cunning, by craftiness in deceitful schemes. Rather, speaking the truth in love, we are to grow up in every way into him who is the head, into Christ, from whom the whole body, joined and held together by every joint with which it is equipped, when each part is working properly, makes the body grow so that it builds itself up in love. (Eph 4:11-16)

You can see in this passage how good teachers promote growth in the church. They "equip the saints for the work of ministry" and help protect people from being tricked by false teaching.[2] Growth also leads to love and unity within the church. This passage has that beautiful image of the church as a body working together in love with each part doing its work.

Teaching is not about disseminating abstract 'head knowledge'. It's God's way of promoting endurance, encouragement, service, unity and love within the body of Christ. So being able to teach matters for Growth Group leaders.

2   The word 'ministry' in Ephesians 4:12 has a sense of bringing God's revelation to others (e.g. v. 15 "speaking the truth in love"). So it's not the case that the leaders do the word ministry and others are just recipients who are equipped to serve in other ways. The leaders prepare all Christians to bring the truth of the gospel to others. The truth of this is seldom more significant than in the context of Growth Groups. For more on this, see Lionel Windsor, 'The Work of Ministry in Ephesians 4:12', *GoThereFor.com*, 13 October 2016: www.gotherefor.com/offer. php?intid=29471

Growing in our ability to teach

Some people are naturally good at teaching—they seem to make learning fun and easy. In fact, teaching is listed as a gift in Romans 12:7. But we can all grow in this ability. It may be that this is a gift we can pick up with a bit of training and practice.

The best way to grow as a teacher is actually to grow in our character and knowledge of God (the first two core competencies). This will help us to teach people wisely in our group from a position of love and humility. So it's worth going back to those chapters and continuing to reflect on our growth in those areas.

When it comes to teaching more specifically there are a few things we can do to grow:

1. **Get trained.** Getting trained makes immediate sense. There's a course called *Growth Groups* by Col Marshall (Matthias Media) that has been around for years and has been used to train thousands of leaders. It's the course that trained me in how to lead a Growth Group and I still use principles from it today. In the course manual there are some great chapters on teaching. Ideally you'd do this course in a small group format so you can get experience in leading studies. If that's not possible then it's still worth working through the manual by yourself or with one of your pastors. Matthias Media has also published a more recent course, *The Small Group and the Vine*, which sets the vision for Growth Group leading and takes you through the basic skills of teaching the Bible in a Growth Group setting. And finally, I've written another short book called *Writing a Small Group Study*, which is especially helpful if you have never written Bible studies before.

2. **Teach individuals.** Another way you can grow as a teacher is to meet one-to-one with another Christian (ideally someone who's younger than you in Christian experience and maturity) to read the Bible and pray. This experience is good for so many reasons, but one of them is that it forces you to repeatedly ask questions, respond to answers and explain what you're reading. These are great skills for teaching a Growth Group.

   It's usually not hard to find someone to read the Bible with. If you need any help just ask one of your pastors. Churches will sometimes provide training in this, and there's a great short book you can look at by David Helm called *One-to-One Bible Reading* (Matthias Media).

3. **Teach groups.** The third way to grow as a teacher is to teach groups of people. This will not only give you practice at explaining things, you'll also learn how to relate to a mixed group of people of different levels of understanding. Here are a few ways to get experience teaching groups:

   - *Teach children:* There are heaps of opportunities for teaching in children's ministry. You could teach a Sunday children's class or get involved in youth or children's ministries during the week. Children's ministry is great for forcing us to explain the Bible clearly and simply. Even if you can't commit regularly, it's worth volunteering for holiday kids' class opportunities.
   - *Teach your Growth Group:* If you're already in a Growth Group, speak with your current leader and ask if you can have a go at leading the group sometime. They can help you prepare the study, observe you, and give you feedback afterwards.

- *Give a Bible talk:* This might feel like a big step, but it's a great experience for teaching the Bible. In a small church you might have the opportunity to preach on Sunday. Otherwise there are often opportunities at kids' or youth ministry. You can speak with your pastor if you'd like to give it a go.

Conclusion

These are just a few ways in which you can grow in your ability to teach. As always, this is a good thing to pray about. We also need to continue to remember God's grace as we try, fail or succeed in this process. Be encouraged that growing as a teacher will be a great blessing for God's church and for the people in your group.

Questions

- Why is it important that leaders be able to teach?

- How are you going with the four qualities seen in competent teachers?

- How can you get some experience and training?

- Growing in a skill can sometimes lead to pride. How can you grow in humility even as you grow in your teaching skills?

- Write down some goals for growing in your ability to teach.

Goal	Plan	Time period

4. Encouragement of others

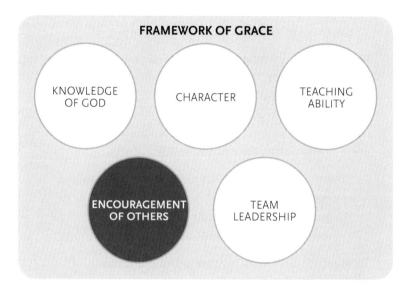

FRAMEWORK OF GRACE

KNOWLEDGE OF GOD

CHARACTER

TEACHING ABILITY

ENCOURAGEMENT OF OTHERS

TEAM LEADERSHIP

The first three core competencies of Growth Group leading seem pretty obvious. Character, knowledge of God and teaching ability are all clearly necessary for a fruitful Growth Group ministry. The next two—encouragement of others and team leadership—are not so obvious. In this chapter we look at the first of these and see why competency in this area is essential for Growth Group leading.

At the outset, it's important to be clear that when we talk about 'encouragement', we don't necessarily mean saying nice things to someone. In his book *Encouragement: How Words Change Lives*, Gordon Cheng helpfully defines encouragement for us:

Christian encouragement is speaking the truth in love, with the aim of building Christians up in Christlikeness, as we wait for the day of judgement. Christian encouragement will likewise involve speaking the truth in love to unbelievers, thus encouraging them to put their trust in Christ for forgiveness and salvation.[3]

In other words, encouragement is spurring people on to keep (or begin) following Jesus. It could be through words of comfort, admonition or exhortation.

The most important encouragement ministry comes from God—Father, Son and Spirit. These two passages from Acts and 2 Thessalonians show this well:

Then the church throughout Judea, Galilee and Samaria enjoyed a time of peace and was strengthened. Living in the fear of the Lord and encouraged by the Holy Spirit, it increased in numbers. (Acts 9:31, NIV)[4]

May our Lord Jesus Christ himself and God our Father, who loved us and by his grace gave us eternal encouragement and good hope, encourage your hearts and strengthen you in every good deed and word. (2 Thess 2:16-17, NIV)

God is the ultimate encourager and we always need to be looking to him for encouragement. However, the Bible also says encouraging others is something for all Christians to be doing.

3   Gordon Cheng, *Encouragement: How Words Change Lives*, Matthias Media, Sydney, 2006, p. 13.
4   The Greek word for 'encourage' can be translated in a few different ways, such as 'exhort' or 'comfort'. These options bring out different aspects of the word. For simplicity, in parts of this chapter I've chosen the NIV translation where 'encourage' is used more consistently. The same goes for the noun 'encouragement'.

This is one of the big themes of Hebrews:

> But encourage one another daily, as long as it is called "Today", so that none of you may be hardened by sin's deceitfulness. (Heb 3:13, NIV)

> And let us consider how to stir up one another to love and good works, not neglecting to meet together, as is the habit of some, but encouraging one another, and all the more as you see the Day drawing near. (Heb 10:24-25)

Some people might be particularly good at encouragement (it is listed as a spiritual gift—"exhortation"—in Romans 12:8) but that doesn't mean the rest of us shouldn't be doing our best.

Although encouragement is a ministry for all Christians, the Bible does stress that it is a particular responsibility for leaders. Paul and Barnabas (whose name means 'son of encouragement', as Acts 4:36 explains) went to the new churches in Asia for this very purpose:

> When they had preached the gospel to that city and had made many disciples, they returned to Lystra and to Iconium and to Antioch, strengthening the souls of the disciples, encouraging them to continue in the faith, and saying that through many tribulations we must enter the kingdom of God. (Acts 14:21-22)

You can see in these verses how they are encouraging suffering Christians to persevere and "continue in the faith". Sometimes Paul couldn't go personally to encourage churches. In those cases he sent his fellow workers to do this. So, for example, Timothy was sent to the Thessalonians to encourage them:

> We sent Timothy, who is our brother and co-worker
> in God's service in spreading the gospel of Christ, to
> strengthen and encourage you in your faith, so that no-
> one would be unsettled by these trials. For you know quite
> well that we are destined for them. (1 Thess 3:2-3, NIV)

Tychicus was another leader Paul sent to encourage churches. He sent him to Ephesus (Eph 6:21-22) and to Colossae (Col 4:7-8) for this purpose.

Paul also commanded Titus to encourage people in Crete:

> These, then, are the things you should teach. Encourage
> and rebuke with all authority. Do not let anyone despise
> you. (Titus 2:15, NIV)

This repeated emphasis on encouragement shows us that it is an important part of Christian ministry, and leaders in the church are expected to be able to do it. That's why it's one of the core competencies of Growth Group leading.

But as we've seen, it's definitely more than giving people a warm smile and a hug now and again. In the Bible, encouragement involves urging people on to keep following Jesus. Sometimes it's about comforting and caring for people who are down and struggling:

> And we urge you, brothers, admonish the idle,
> encourage the fainthearted, help the weak, be patient
> with them all. (1 Thess 5:14)

This includes people who might be suffering for their faith, as we saw in the example above from 1 Thessalonians 3:2-3.

At other times, encouraging involves challenging people over sin. This is where admonishing or gently rebuking people is necessary:

> Preach the word; be prepared in season and out of
> season; correct, rebuke and encourage—with great
> patience and careful instruction. (2 Tim 4:2, NIV)

This is often the scary side of encouragement. A good encourager will value someone's walk with Jesus more than their friendship. This means that leaders will sometimes need to risk losing a relationship for the sake of that person's eternal salvation. There's a great phrase in Ephesians 4:15 that sums up encouragement well: 'speaking the truth in love'. We'll always love the people we're encouraging, and we'll express this by being truthful as we speak.

You can see from this how connected encouragement of others is with the core competencies of character, knowledge of God and teaching ability. Encouragement must come from good character if it's going to be effective and not fake. It must come out of a genuine love for other people. Likewise, good encouragers will be people who have a growing knowledge of God. They will be keen to drag people along with them to know God together. Moreover, in the Bible, teaching and encouragement are closely connected. Often encouragement involves reading the Bible together and showing people from the Bible why they should be encouraged.

Even though there are many connections and even overlaps with the other competencies, encouragement of others is worth considering on its own. Partly this is because of the attention given to encouragement in the Bible. Another reason is that sometimes people realize that they are doing reasonably well on those first three competencies, but not so well here. They might be slowly maturing in their character and know their Bible quite well and even be competent teachers, yet they are not actively encouraging other people. They are too caught up in their own world and the world of immediate friends and family. They aren't actually going out of their way to find and encourage more Christian brothers and sisters. In other cases people can be lovely but actually quite shy. This shyness can make encouraging others a hard thing to do. So looking at encouragement on its own can help us identify potential areas for growth.

So what will it look like to be competent in the area of encouraging others? Here's a list of things that someone gifted in encouragement might be doing:

- thinking about other Christians during the week
- praying for other Christians during the week
- encouraging Christians during the week with things like texts, phone calls or catch ups
- trying to be helpful members of their own Growth Group
- turning up early to church
- speaking with new people or people who are by themselves at church
- being thoughtful about body language and facial expressions as they relate to people
- appropriately moving to conversation about how people are going in their Christian life (e.g. "That was a great sermon; what did you find encouraging from it?" or "How are you going with that thing I promised to pray about last week?")
- meeting one-to-one regularly with one or more people during the week (with Bible reading and prayer as part of this time).

It's a long list, but there's probably more you could add. Hopefully at church there will be lots of people doing this encouragement ministry in all sorts of ways, many of them unnoticed by others.

Growing in encouragement of others

Just like the other core competencies, this is an area we can and should be growing in. So how can we become better encouragers? Most of the time we've already got the skills and we just need to be disciplined and get on with it. The list above is a good place to start. Once we start encouraging others we'll pretty soon gain experience and get better at it.

Sometimes it's helpful to identify our own barriers to encouraging others. These can be very diverse, ranging from shyness to arrogance. For example, if we are really nervous about approaching people then we'll never go up and talk with them. Or if we are too proud, we won't 'lower ourselves' by talking with struggling Christians in our church. These barriers can be pretty deep-seated and are often connected with subconscious fears. It's impossible to address these barriers in a short book like this. The best thing would be to talk with your pastor and say, "I find it hard to encourage people. Can you help me work out why?" This might open up a few issues, but it's worth it if you can be of better use to God.

There's also a great book called *Encouragement: The Key to Caring* by Larry Crabb and Dan Allender (Zondervan). This book looks at what makes a good encourager and how our fears can get in the way. It would be worth reading with someone else and talking about the ideas each chapter raises. Another great book is the one I mentioned at the beginning of this chapter—*Encouragement: How Words Change Lives* by Gordon Cheng.

A note on evangelism

So far we've been talking mainly about encouraging Christians, but there's definitely a place for encouraging non-Christians to consider where they stand with Jesus too. The same love and care we have for our Christian brothers and sisters should overflow to those who are yet to know him at all. The Bible tells us to "walk in wisdom toward outsiders, making the best use of the time" (Col 4:5).

Evangelism might not be a particular gift for Growth Group leaders, but working at it will have a great impact in encouraging others in our groups. It's very hard to urge others to share the news of Jesus if we are not making some effort in this area ourselves.

Conclusion

Encouragement of others might not be the most obvious necessary competency for Growth Group leading, but as we read the Bible we quickly see how important it is. Spurring people on to keep following Jesus is a ministry with great value and eternal consequences. Whether or not you are currently leading, growth in this area will be of great benefit to the people you know and serve.

Questions

•   In your own words, what is encouragement?

- Have a look at that list of things an encouraging person might be doing. Are there things you'd like to try or do more of?

- What do you think might be some of the barriers preventing you from being more encouraging?

- How do you feel about rebuking someone (in love)?

- Write down some goals for growing in your encouragement of others.

Goal	Plan	Time period

Being a Small Group Leader

5. Team leadership

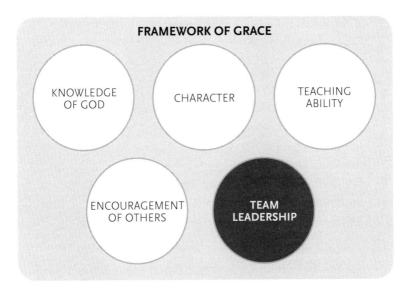

FRAMEWORK OF GRACE

KNOWLEDGE OF GOD

CHARACTER

TEACHING ABILITY

ENCOURAGEMENT OF OTHERS

TEAM LEADERSHIP

Team leadership is the last of the five core competencies. Leadership and its terminology are big topics, but what I mean by team leadership is the capacity to lead others as part of a team within the church. This involves not only leading your Growth Group, but also working alongside other Growth Group leaders and submitting to pastors and leaders who are over you. And in all this we remember that Jesus is the ultimate leader of our church, or the "chief Shepherd" as Peter puts it (1 Peter 5:4).

Leading others

In some ways the capacity to lead others seems almost too obvious to mention. A competent leader needs to lead. The question really is what will that leadership look like? So it's definitely worth mentioning. Paul tells the elders from Ephesus to *be shepherds* even though they are in that role already:

> "Pay careful attention to yourselves and to all the flock, in which the Holy Spirit has made you overseers, to care for the church of God, which he obtained with his own blood." (Acts 20:28)

Shepherding means lovingly leading others and the competent Growth Group leader should be able to do this.

Competency in the other four core areas is definitely an important part of exercising leadership. Character is crucial because people lead by setting an example. Also, a leader's knowledge of God and capacity to teach will help people respect them and listen to them. Lastly, their ability to encourage will mean that people will want to be around them. Some of these qualities come together in a great verse from Hebrews:

> Remember your leaders, who spoke to you the word of God. Consider the outcome of their way of life, and imitate their faith. (Heb 13:7)

Leadership clearly has lots of links to the other four areas of competency.

However, leadership in and of itself is more than those qualities. There's something about leaders that inspires people to follow them. Leading requires a certain degree of confidence and relational ability. Leaders need to be able to overcome their own fears for the sake of the people they are leading. Often this is the fear of what other people think or a strong desire to please them. A good leader will put these aside and be concerned solely about pleasing the person he serves: Jesus. Paul compares a leader to a soldier wanting to please his commanding officer:

Being a Small Group Leader

Share in suffering as a good soldier of Christ Jesus. No
soldier gets entangled in civilian pursuits, since his aim
is to please the one who enlisted him. (2 Tim 2:3-4)

Being competent in team leadership also requires reliability
and dependability. Paul trusts Timothy in this, as someone who
has proved himself:

I hope in the Lord Jesus to send Timothy to you soon,
so that I too may be cheered by news of you. For I have
no-one like him, who will be genuinely concerned for
your welfare. For they all seek their own interests, not
those of Jesus Christ. But you know Timothy's proven
worth, how as a son with a father he has served with me
in the gospel. (Phil 2:19-22)

A leader should be organized and capable of managing a group
of people. So Paul says to Timothy about leaders:

He must manage his own household well, with all
dignity keeping his children submissive, for if someone
does not know how to manage his own household, how
will he care for God's church? (1 Tim 3:4-5)

This management side of things would include mundane
activities like being able to be at Growth Group on time and
relatively prepared. A leader should be able to gather people
and do things like organize a social event or fulfil a roster
commitment.

Leading with others

Leadership also involves being able to lead with others. Often
this means working with a co-leader. A good leader will be able
to communicate well with their co-leader and include them in
shepherding the group. For women co-leading mixed groups

this will mean being able to respect their male co-leader (even if he's less experienced than they are).[5] For a man co-leading with a woman, it will mean finding biblically appropriate ways for the woman to shepherd the group with him. At the very least, it will mean seeking her wise counsel on how to grow the people in the group.

Within a church a good leader should have generosity towards other groups and Growth Group leaders. They certainly won't be competitive and want to be 'the most popular group' for the sake of their self-esteem.

Submitting to other leaders

Finally, leadership involves submitting to leaders and pastors who are in authority over us.

Submission is a virtue for every Christian. Even Jesus submitted to his parents (Luke 2:51) and to his heavenly Father (Luke 22:42). Paul tells us all to "[submit] to one another out of reverence for Christ" (Eph 5:21). Submission simply means respecting and obeying people who are in a position of authority over us.

Within the church, we are all called to submit to leaders who take responsibility for us:

> Obey your leaders and submit to them, for they are
> keeping watch over your souls, as those who will have
> to give an account. Let them do this with joy and not
> with groaning, for that would be of no advantage to you.
> (Heb 13:17)

5   It's important for Growth Group leaders and co-leaders to come to grips with the Bible's teaching on the roles of men and women in church contexts. I strongly recommend that you read Claire Smith's book, *God's Good Design* (Matthias Media) on this topic.

For Growth Group leaders this means submitting to the leadership of the church, and working well with the pastor(s) responsible for small groups. It means cheerfully following their leadership and doing what they ask. Some Growth Group leaders have great leadership qualities and will perhaps end up leading churches themselves one day. But for now they need to be part of a team.

This doesn't mean that leaders will never disagree with their pastors or the direction of the church. But respectful leaders will gently and politely raise their concerns privately with the pastors, rather than grumble to their group or promote a spirit of disunity among group members. Ideally group members will perceive that their Growth Group leader loves their church and is enthusiastic about what's going on.

Growing in team leadership

There are various ways we can be growing in this core competency of team leadership.

To lead others well we need to grow in confidence and overcome our fears. This can happen through formal Growth Group training and growing in the other four areas of competency. It will be helpful to try to identify your fears and talk these through with your pastor.

We also grow as leaders by leading in contexts other than in Growth Groups. This could be with your family and children or among your flatmates. It could also be within other ministries around church that require leadership. Becoming increasingly capable in these ministries is a good indication of capability for the leadership side of Growth Group ministries.

If organization and reliability aren't your strong points, it's worth growing in these areas as well. There are various resources on getting more organized—for example, *Getting*

Things Done by David Allen (Penguin). Most people will do well just by keeping a diary and making lists of things to do.

Growing in submission sometimes requires a bit of reflection. If you're unhappy about something at church, you need to figure out if it's no big deal (in which case you should let it go) or if it's something that's likely to continue to trouble you. If it's an ongoing thing, you need to gently raise it privately with one of your pastors. If you've been guilty of grumbling about church or promoting disunity you need to repent and potentially straighten things out.

Finally, there's a great book on leadership by Craig Hamilton called *Wisdom in Leadership* (Matthias Media). This has 78 short chapters on pretty much every aspect of leadership. Reading this (and perhaps even discussing the chapters with a friend or pastor) would be a great help in your leadership growth.

Conclusion

To sum up, Growth Group leaders need to be competent in team leadership. They need to be able to lead others, work with fellow leaders and submit to the pastors at church. Hopefully, under the ultimate leadership of Jesus, they will help people mature in Christ and bring glory to God.

Questions

- What is team leadership about?

- How are you going with showing leadership in your home life (e.g. among your family or flatmates)? Do you contribute to the household? Are you setting an example?

- How are you going at work or uni? Are you able to organize yourself and reliably complete the tasks you're given?

- How are you going at respecting and submitting to church leaders? Have you been grumbling about things to others?

- In what ways are you leading others at church? Are there opportunities to grow and improve this ministry?

- What fears do you have, especially about leading? Who can you talk to about these?

- Write down some goals for growing in your team leadership.

Goal	Plan	Time period

Being a Small Group Leader

6. Being a competent Growth Group leader

So where to from here? Having thought through the five core competencies of Growth Group leading you could be experiencing a variety of emotions. Perhaps you're excited about the prospect of setting goals and growing in some of these areas. Or perhaps being reminded of your weaknesses has left you discouraged. Maybe it's a mix of both. This chapter will help you figure out your next steps.

The grace of God

This is an excellent time to reflect again on the grace of God:

> For we ourselves were once foolish, disobedient, led astray, slaves to various passions and pleasures, passing our days in malice and envy, hated by others and hating one another. But when the goodness and loving kindness of God our Saviour appeared, he saved us, not because of works done by us in righteousness, but according to his own mercy, by the washing of regeneration and renewal of the Holy Spirit, whom he poured out on us richly through Jesus Christ our Saviour, so that being justified by his grace we might become heirs according to the hope of eternal life. (Titus 3:3-7)

Our salvation wasn't the result of our righteous works but because of God's mercy. We live in a relationship of grace with our heavenly Father, mediated through Jesus Christ our

Saviour. Likewise, our ministry is not about our good works but about God's grace. God is the one who grows us and uses us in ministry for his purposes:

> What then is Apollos? What is Paul? Servants through whom you believed, as the Lord assigned to each.
> (1 Cor 3:5)

So don't despair if you're aware of your weaknesses in ministry! Our salvation is secure in Christ and God will use us as he wants. The best thing you can do is take those feelings of inadequacy and turn them into prayers to God. Ask him for growth in all those areas and ask him that you might be useful for his purposes in the world.

In the same way, don't be proud if you are competent in any of these areas. Any growth we have is from God:

> For who sees anything different in you? What do you have that you did not receive? If then you received it, why do you boast as though you did not receive it?
> (1 Cor 4:7)

If you do have some competency in these areas then the best thing to do is thank God and ask him for humility. Pray also that he might show you areas where you can continue to grow.

Growing in the five core competencies

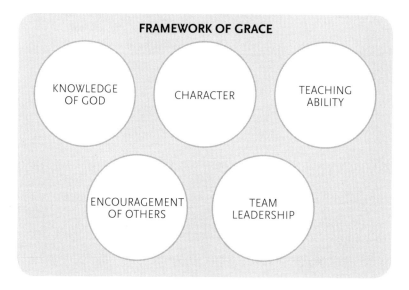

Having reflected again on God's grace, we're in a good place to think again about growing in these five areas. Hopefully by now you've got a good grasp of what they are and why they are important in Growth Group leading. You should also have tried to answer the questions at the end of the chapters (if not, take time to go back and do this). You might have a longish list of things you need to do or change. Now is a good time to try and figure out what the most important two or three of these are. Long lists of goals can be overwhelming, so you're better off working on two or three and then revisiting this book in a few months and picking more goals to work on. Here's some space to write down a few goals (with one example):

Competency	Goal	Plan	Time period
Character	Stop swearing	Pray; confess to a friend; stop doing it.	Change today. Review with friend in a month.

Being a Small Group Leader

Starting to lead

It's also time to think about whether you actually can and should start Growth Group leading. What factors go into this decision? There are several to consider.

Fortunately, leaders and pastors are the ones who take responsibility for appointing Growth Group leaders. It's not normally a ministry you just start yourself. Paul tells pastors:

> Do not be hasty in the laying on of hands, nor take part
> in the sins of others; keep yourself pure. (1 Tim 5:22)

So, firstly, ask your pastors whether they think you're ready to lead and be ready to respect their opinion.

Secondly, even if you're competent to lead, there might not be a need for you to do so at this particular time at your church. It might be that God has provided a great bunch of leaders for now, and the real need is in another ministry. That may be a ministry you're less enthusiastic about. In this case, it's time to remember that we are a body and what matters is not our own preferences but the building of the body:

> For by the grace given to me I say to everyone among
> you not to think of himself more highly than he ought
> to think, but to think with sober judgement, each
> according to the measure of faith that God has assigned.
> For as in one body we have many members, and the
> members do not all have the same function, so we,
> though many, are one body in Christ, and individually
> members one of another. (Rom 12:3-5)

So ideally you'll be saying to your pastor, "I'm happy to lead a group if that's where I'm needed, but if not, just tell me where you'd like me to serve and I'll do my best".

Thirdly, even if you're competent to lead, you may or may

not have the capacity to lead at this particular time. All sorts of things can impinge on our capacity to lead. This could include mental or physical health, family relationships (including children), or work and university commitments. Sometimes it's hard to judge what's a difficulty and what's a deal breaker. Fortunately this is something you can work through with your pastors. They should be able to chat with you about your life with a bit more objectivity. Sometimes they'll be able to figure out ways of overcoming barriers or challenges to the practicalities of leading.

So that's where we finish. I hope you've been challenged to grow and serve God in growing Christians to maturity.

At the beginning of this book, I made the comment that there are a bunch of reasons that Growth Groups shouldn't work. Yet, in God's grace, and generally through prayerful and 'competent' leadership, they actually *do* seem to work— people in Growth Groups grow in Christ over time. What a magnificently God-glorifying and Christ-honouring endeavour for his people to be involved in. May God strengthen you as you seek to serve him in this way.

Questions

- Do you feel competent to lead? Who can you talk to about this?

- Do you think you are able to lead at this time if required? What are some of the challenges that would be good to talk through with a pastor?

Feedback on this resource

We really appreciate getting feedback about our resources—not just suggestions for how to improve them, but also positive feedback and ways they can be used. We especially love to hear that the resources may have helped someone in their Christian growth.

You can send feedback to us via the 'Feedback' menu in our online store, or write to us at info@matthiasmedia.com.au.

matthiasmedia

Matthias Media is an evangelical publishing ministry that seeks to persuade all Christians of the truth of God's purposes in Jesus Christ as revealed in the Bible, and equip them with high-quality resources, so that by the work of the Holy Spirit they will:

- abandon their lives to the honour and service of Christ in daily holiness and decision-making
- pray constantly in Christ's name for the fruitfulness and growth of his gospel
- speak the Bible's life-changing word whenever and however they can—in the home, in the world and in the fellowship of his people.

Our wide range of resources includes Bible studies, books, training courses, tracts and children's material. To find out more, and to access samples and free downloads, visit our website:

www.matthiasmedia.com

How to buy our resources

1. Direct from us over the internet:
   – in the US: www.matthiasmedia.com
   – in Australia: www.matthiasmedia.com.au

2. Direct from us by phone: please visit our website for current phone contact information.

3. Through a range of outlets in various parts of the world. Visit **www.matthiasmedia.com/contact** for details about recommended retailers in your part of the world.

4. Trade enquiries can be addressed to:
   – in the US and Canada: sales@matthiasmedia.com
   – in Australia and the rest of the world: sales@matthiasmedia.com.au

Register at our website for our **free** regular email update to receive information about the latest new resources, **exclusive special offers**, and free articles to help you grow in your Christian life and ministry.

Writing a Small Group Study

By Richard Sweatman

The Bible study you write for your small group can result in an exhilarating journey that opens God's word up and leads people to grow and change. It can also be a hard slog that seems to have little impact on anyone.

If you're hoping for the former but worried you'll end up with the latter, this book is for you.

Putting together a faithful and illuminating Bible study might seem like a huge task, but in *Writing a Small Group Study* Richard Sweatman breaks that task down into clear and achievable steps that won't overwhelm you. He carefully explains how to work your way through each step to create a study that will engage your small group with God's powerful word.

This book is a superb guide for the new small group leader, as well as an excellent refresher for those who have been leading for years.

Richard Sweatman has been the maturity pastor at Hunter Bible Church and UniChurch in Newcastle, NSW, for the past 10 years. He spends his time training and equipping leaders in small group ministry.

FOR MORE INFORMATION OR TO ORDER CONTACT:

Matthias Media
Email: sales@matthiasmedia.com.au
www.matthiasmedia.com.au

Matthias Media (USA)
Email: sales@matthiasmedia.com
www.matthiasmedia.com

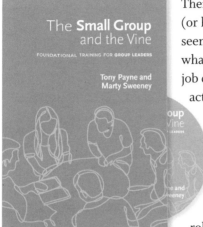